may god
help us
find our
way.

MAY GOD
HELP US
FIND
OUR WAY

reyna biddy

dedications
for the women who came before me
and taught me about the work . for
the men who came around when i
longed for warmth. for the questions
we still desire an answer to. for the
love i was promised by god. for the
country i belong to the most. for
the spirits that guide me toward an
arousing place. for the euphoric
memories of delusion. for the
disappointment i've compartmentalized.
for the disbelief i still feel. for the
distortion of my child hood. for
the conclusions i've come to find
on my own. for the results—that
led me here.   asking more.

contents

introduction:

I've been thinking about a home;
some place to call our own. Somewhere nice..
a long way from here. Beneath the surface—
waiting to be cracked. In between the rainbow.
Right at the center of dark and light.. or water
and lightening. Above the horizon, while the
moon sets and while the sun is rising. At the
beginning of hope and at the end of fear. There
are no worries here. I hear the journey is lucid
and less painful. Somewhere, more alluring than
a daydream. Where the site is more engaging than
each thought in the back of our minds. Some
place abundant, some place golden. A resort for
both, you and i. you know? A heaven that will
not intimidate us for living our lives and a God
who accepts us without judgment first. Here
there is no conviction—here there is no venom.
Here, we are all welcome to be who we were
set out to be. Here we are loved unconditionally;
Here—we are too in love; to believe love
is anything less than unconditional.

one: blood

1.   i am here on the behalf of women. i am here
     on the behalf of blood. i am here on the
     behalf of birth. i am here on the behalf of
     breath. i am here on the behalf of stretch
     marks—hidden, or bare, and unconcealed. i
     am here on the behalf of stomach's who
     hang over waist lines; who hide in the face of
     attention. i am here on the behalf of sagging
     arms and swollen nipples. i am here on the
     behalf of failure. in like manner, i am here on
     the behalf of visibly caged ribs. i am here on
     the behalf of impatience and mistrust. i am
     here on the behalf of impractical
     expectations. i am here on the behalf of
     aesthetic intentions. i am here on the behalf
     of hunger. i am dehydrated here. i am here
     helpless. i am here to say i'm sorry. i am here
     because i see no other way. i am here to say i
     gave my all.   i am here to say   will
     you   forgive me?

2. i suppose you don't want to take notice of
    my truth.   all, foul and alarming like. all
    emotive and impulsive. speaking too loud
    and too sincere. is my essence too bright a
    light amongst your somber course? are my
    scars too pure for you? can you see them
    glow in the dark? does your skin crawl at the
    honesty of them? oh.. how they'll creep out
    their rusty bronzed casket and sneak up the
    vines to your heart. do they make you feel a
    way?   do they take you back; to a place you
    thought you'd forgotten? do they remind
    you of your malice? or your trauma? or your
    guilt? this is for real. this reflection, this echo
    —is for real. this is your fixed subconscious
    that controls your every move. this was for
    the higher conscience you claimed to have.
    my existence. your indifference. my silence.
    your pride.   my hurt.   can you see
    what you've made of me?

3. i am here on the behalf of blackness. i am
    here on the behalf of darkened skin. i am
    here on the behalf of melanin. i am here on

the behalf of the sun—my friend. i am here
on the behalf of naps and puffy lips. i am
here on the behalf of every insecurity you
gave me. i am here on the behalf of
disillusion. i am here on the behalf of
oppression. i am here on the behalf of
rhythm.   watch,   as my hips sway from
left to right.. at the answer of each prayer.
and in your case, preyer.

4.   aren't i blessed to be in your presence?
      haven't i greeted you with enough grace? are
      you here to celebrate my survival? won't you
      celebrate with me? i needn't let you forget;
      i am here for the blues you took from me.
      and the jazz, and the spoken word poetry,
      and the magic, and the despair.   the
      revelation, too. i am here on the behalf of a
      dark skinned jesus.   i am here on the
      behalf of voodoo. i am here on the behalf of
      art and clairvoyance and spirit. i am here on
      the behalf of karma.   i am here to say
      thank god.   i mustn't forget   to
      thank a white god for you.

5. suppose i spoke back at you, or lashed at you,
    or laughed at you, or whipped you into
    position, or disagreed and disregarded your
    opinions. suppose i sowed the devil in your
    backyard, right underneath your feet. right
    where i promised the grass would be all the
    more greener. or suppose i took your father
    from home to work for me or to fight for
    me. or to serve life—for, the reflection of my
    sins. suppose i took him for granted.
    granted,   he owes me this.   he showed
    me this.

6. i am here on the behalf of red. i am here on
    the behalf of barriers and language.
    i am here on the behalf of
    miscommunication and cuidado.   i am
    here on the behalf of laboring hands.
    i am here on the behalf of díos.   i am
    here on the behalf of olive toned skin.
    i am here as la negríta; sol y luna tambien.
    por favor, let us in.
    we are here   to support you.

7. let us sprinkle our faith into the cracks of you. the ones broken for good—if you still believe in being saved; 　and if you still believe in healing.
8. i heard them say, "god don't like ugly." and so, i figure by now you know—there's no room for flaws. let us help you.
9. let us boil herbal leaves and flowers before you spread your wings again.. let us help you get away from the cancer. help us take the cancer out of you. let us put this soul work to use. let us show you where the illness lays, let us defeat it with our faith and our bare hands. let us compliment you with a rebirth.
10. maybe, 　then—you will love me. 　maybe then you will let me fly into the starry night with you. 　maybe when i'm ready to surrender. 　or maybe when i demand more..
11. i am here in search for freedom. in search for a wind with a cool breeze. in search for the perfect kind of sand to sink my toes in. 　in search for the waves that will cleanse me. that will purify my reputation. in search for a

home. a little something to call my own,
every now and again.   something i can brag
about.   for me and my people.

12. no.. i don't need your approval nor want
your hand out.. i just want to let you know
some things.   all this time,   all this polite
you stole from me.   today, i'm claiming it
back. i'm turning over a new slate and
stepping into my destiny;   where you no
longer belong. there is no more you to haunt
me. i've saged your ghosts away. i've purified
my space. moving at my own pace. speaking
whenever, if ever, i feel it fit to. i'm finding it
my way, and don't want to be held back by
your bones or your make believe suffering.
but i will say, be careful.   not
all things   forget.

13. that ego gon' kill you, if fate doesn't.

14. and one   day,   by the grace of god,
we will find our way back — to each other..
without you.

two: a grandma who wonders

"Que paso?"
She asked.

      Nothing.
      and everything
      at once.

      "Nothing loves me back."
      i whispered.

She looked at me confused.
She looked at me amused.
She smiled.

"Look around you.
There's love everywhere.
There's a blue in the sky.
There's a promise in the air.
There's a bird chirping.   can't you hear it?

There are trees to help you grow more patient.
There's healing—there's hope..
There's everything / you forgot."

"But none of it is for me.
None of this beauty."

"If not for you,
for who?"

"For someone   who deserves it."

"And you
 deserve it
the most."

three: warrior   women

As i sit.. i watch you soft, and
unbothered, while you sharpen your sword.
while you sing a psalm, on your front porch,
about the lord's love and heaven's gates. as you
wave to every person passing. as you give thanks
for every person passing. as you share love with
every person pleased to take. while you hum the
most beautiful hum. believe the most freeing
promise. believing every thing will be okay. as
regular as they always are. as innocent as they've
ever felt.   you're surrounded by festivity and
fright.   the war is near.   you haven't a
fear in the world.

— You welcome in the turmoil
you feel we're prepared for.

—

I watch as the sweat drip from around your left eye. no squint, or concern. sharper.. it has to be sharper. hands as hard as rocks. smile as temporary as morning. hair half baked from the day's sunlight. faith that measures from here—to —passed the moon. or from here to wherever the ocean begins or ends at. while the damp evaporate, you never dared to wipe your cheek.. as though your effort deserved all the recognition it could get; or it would find itself feeling forgotten. no one pays attention in the calm. no one wanting to face the truth. behind the scenes of battle—there was me and there was you.   and there was a god we both thought we knew.

— Patiently waiting for the storm.
gathering our weapons and our devotion.

—

Do we serve a god
who tests our devotion?
do we deserve to live this way?
to never know the difference
between karma and the next phase?
to never know the difference
between tragedy and mistake?
to never know the difference
between luck and fortune?
to never know where we'll go
next.

they said we were fortunate to be here.
they said we were burdens, and to leave here.

— They said we were crying too much.
they said we were speaking too often.
Said we'd live a lifetime working
underneath 'em.

—

It's been a few lifetimes—i been working.
he been working. she been working.
we been working against each other.
we've never worked together.

this is what you wanted right?
to steal our freedom?
to live off our thoughts and ideas?
to make us believe our body's
are only ever beautiful
once they become corpses?

— I see you for what you are.
you're, "sorry that it's been so hard."
that it's been this long.
that it still hasn't gone away.
that you like us best when we're helpless.
that you think it's best we remain hopeless.
i know,   "you're sorry."

four: know this.

I wanted to start this poem by saying,
"Steve.. i'm ashamed of you."
or "Steve.. shame on you."
But i took it upon myself to hold conviction.
Rather let you know my issues,
whether you listen or not.
See,   we're not in the same   battle
and we're not   fighting the   same   war,
and as tired as i am, by the end of each day
i will still find a way to be an amenity for you.
i will still lend what's left of my   vitality
to hold   your spirit   in place.

Do you feel okay today?

i can't afford to lose you
to the battle you're fighting.
Even if i don't feel so passionate today.
i can't afford not to smile.

It's much bigger than the both of us / know.
But please, remember,
you're not fighting for us.
You're fighting for you,
and i'm dying for you.

I'm doing my best to avoid your anger,
so i can wake up in the morning equipped.
Ready—to send you off
into what you believe to be
'a kind of life.'

A life that only the white man can provide.
What makes him more worthy of love?
Why pretend to be complete for them?
            Yet,
You share your demons with me.
You fall apart when it comes to me.

Is this all i'm deserving of?
Your tainted fragments?

You see how hard it is
for me to live my own life,
don't you?

How hard it is for me to get out of bed.
How easy it is for me to lye down.
How can they see me for who i am,
if you don't?

i'm exhausted.

You told me you knew love.
Is this the capacity of your passion?
Is this all   you have   left for me..
at the moment?

Will there be more of you
at another time?

five: my   god   said

Come here.
Let me untwist your hair,
n massage your head..
Let me, pick your brain.
i wanna let you in
to this safe space
i hold and keep
sacred for you.

i know "your kind" of hurt.
i kinda wish i could take
the pain away from you.
i seen how the devil likes to
have his way with you.
i felt their hate for you.
Their innate ways to fake
and play with you
and this life you were given.
Or this nightmare you are living.
Pardon 'em for not seeing
your purpose.

But for what it's worth,
we're in this life thing together.

So,
caint you,
love me deeper than that?

Like god intended?
Cant you remember
where you came from?
Like.. you ain't came
from my seed of love.
Your broken spirit can't always
be the excuse. \

Thought i taught you the gravity
of respect
and paying dues.

Thought you knew,   my god
     don't. like, ugly.

My god said she needs an apology.

Needs to know you see
all the beauty she created.

Needs you to know
wouldn't be no 'you',
if it wasn't for us.

    My god said,
     "How much
     harder
    we got
      to love you?"

six: black body

An ode to the black woman's body.
She's been through a lot.
Years and years on end,
she chose to keep on.
To hold on. To love, then, to love again.
Then to lose to love again.

To hug black bodies like it's the last time,
like last time—every time.

To bear baby after baby
praying this time, maybe..
they'll be birthed into safety.
Ideally, a place where someone can love em.

Hoping this time—We can trust each other
enough to tell one another our fears.
i might start by saying, i need you.
When you go.. i'm afraid to let you—
i don't want to survive alone, again.
Our bodies have become too familiar.

With chance.
With each other.
With freedom.

Except never a chance to experience
freedom with each other.

These days, i'm tired
of sharing your body
between the world and me.
So won't you promise,
this time your body
will make it home to me.

To this love.
To this unity.
To this journey
We're supposed to be on together.
Yesterday, tomorrow,
and forever.   Today,
i'll be waiting on our forever after.

*Our body's are tired of
missing you's.

seven: influence

My auntie sunday
said i ain't living right.
Said i should be up
in the skrip clubs,
living it up, living my best life,
letting my hair down—like she do.
Said i'm not living my truth.

i say,
"i don't have the time
or the money."

And she say,
"CHILD!
Don't you worry about money!
You look JUST like me.
You're so pretty, you gon'
make a nigga pray for you.
Gon' make a nigga pay
for your wellbeing
for the rest of his life.

You just gotta make time for him.
You just gotta ask for more;
give more too.
You gotta use your body
the way they want you to.
  You know?"

My mama said,
  "Date someone lighter than you.
They'll give you an opportunity
for something "better."
And almost anything is better
than this black man who helped me make you.
This nigga who trapped me in his web
of disorder.   These nigga's ain't no good.
Come into your life
and suck the light out of you.
Date somebody who can take care of you.
Date somebody who GOT you. for life."

My mama said,
"Umi's color might change."
Hopefully, would change.
   Should,   change.
Said his darkness wasn't so welcoming.
said,   "it's okay..
the winter is coming."

i say, "Mom..
his color is beautiful."

And she say,
"Of course it is,
i'm just saying.
   Imagine?"

                          ‐

My daddy said he loves black women.
Said them white cats up at the job
ain't always treating him right..

Said both his mexican baby mama's
ain't never treating him right.
Said,
   "Shit ain't supposed to be this way."

i say,
"Karma
has her own plans."

My daddy tried his best to love me.
Tried his best to mask his hate for my 'kind'.

See..   daddy's mama   left him
    up at the system.
wasn't worried bout his wellbeing.
went off to start a new family.

Had them white folk up there
feeding him supper.
Had them white folks
holding up his supper.
Let them white folks take advantage.
Daddy's mama just up and left .

My daddy said,
"Black women don't make sense to me.
Black women wasn't meant for me.
Black women might be strong..
but black women are too weak for me.
    Too loud.   Too aggressive.
too aggravating to settle down with.
You see what my black mama did to me?
i thank god you're mixed."

-

My baby daddy said,
"Why're you so aggressive?
Why are you always yelling?
Why're you so demanding all the time?
Why can't you let me be in peace?
Is this your projection   of love?
i really can't tell most the time."

My baby daddy said,
   "Why are you always crying?
   Why are you closed off?
   Why can't we talk like adults?
   Why must you shut down
      so often?
   What do i have to do to make
      you comfortable"

i love my baby daddy,   sometimes,
we just don't see love the same way.
i say "i love you" in different ways;
he wants it in the way he's used to.

            i never known that way.

      i never know what to say..

My folk was never the type
to say "i love you."

            ‑

i said,
i wouldn't let any influences
bring me out my place.
Even if trying to find "my place"
in this world has become too confusing.
i try to love myself,   despite,
and   in spite of,   resentment.
Throughout life i survived
without any   public   display
of affection.   i didn't know any better.
    Or i knew there was better
            in store for me.
i have moved along..
  with perseverance
by the way of intuition.
   i am learning ,
   the meaning of forgiveness.   still.

            -

Most days,   i don't flinch at much.

i never mind
emotional neglect.
  but now..
i'm a   mother   now.

    i can't afford not to love me and my child.

i'm learning the ways of love.
the honest, daring, affectionate, kind.
the kind of love that's larger than for self.

    i gotta show him what his life means to me.

How i'm pose to love
    his black skin
if i haven't
accepted mine?

How
    i'm pose to raise a being
higher   if i can barely
face myself?   if i can hardly let go
   of this person—who was created out of lust.

eight: a reminder.

does your heart feel any better today? is your
capacity to love any larger? what might it take?
anything i can help you set yourself free from? if
it makes a difference, things will get better from
here; but only if you allow it. 'here' meaning the
place you can't seem to get out of. 'allowance'
meaning without blocking blessings. you
shouldn't sit in your sadness—that'll only
manifest more. you shouldn't hold on so tight—
you might confuse your needs with your wants
and forget to abandon those that no longer serve
you any good. stop being stubborn, you don't
need it, or them, anymore. instead of cursing
'em, be grateful for the experience, and wish 'em
well. the less karmic debt, the better. give yourself
time to repair. give yourself space to breathe. it's
probably best you sit alone for a while. let your
thoughts run wild; then learn to still your mind.
many things we have no control over, let's try our
best to guide our thoughts toward a happy place.
all of this as a start, then, let's move accordingly.

nine: world mental health day

1. because i needed an excuse to ask you to excuse me for my behavior.

2. excuse me for my breakdowns that have no birthplace, my anxiety that forces me to stay in—even on nights i promised i'd be there, my insecurities that keep me from loving as deep as you do, my mood swings that ruin everything, my ugly days that reflect my day, my empty that haunts me. my past comes back to haunt me more often than i anticipate. excuse me for not having all the answers, or support, or the emotion you need when all you need is for me to show up for you..

3. because i hardly show up for myself.

4. because today i'm all by myself.

5. because today i feel better.

6. although tonight i'll feel worse.

7. because no one believes me when i'm not feeling well. because i have every reason to.

8. because healing is an everyday process..

9. because for two years, i've been showing no progress.

10. because isolation is selfish.

11. because loving yourself makes the most sense, until you love yourself enough to never want to be around those who don't love you the same way.

12. because no one really loves me the same.

13. because no one really knows the "real" me.

14. because no one cares to learn the "real" me.

15. because those who do make me feel guilty for not being positive enough. or for not looking at the glass half full. or for seeming more blessed than i'm willing to acknowledge. when really, i'm just grateful that i've got the glass in any way.

16. because those who think they know me, think they know what i need. think they know i'm okay. think they know what makes me happy. think they know i'm happy.

17. because those who hold me accountable can't dare to see me this way. can't bare to

find themselves loving someone, or
something, as broken as them.

18. because complaining too much about weight
makes me ridiculous, blind, and ungrateful.

19. because i've eaten myself to exhaustion and
i've starved myself skinny—and still that's
not enough. i want to feel, both, full and
emptier.

20. because fullness is trending. and freedom is
light. the lighter you are the higher you fly.
because flying is free. because i'm tired of
doing things the safe way. because i'd rather
have heavy wings than a heavy heart and a
pair of heavy eyes to match it.

21. because fulfilling dreams only keep me sane
for a moment.

22. because lately i've had these dreams where
the sun's so bright it's blinding. where the
water's rise so high i'm drowning.

23. because maybe.. in real life it's both.

24. maybe i can't breathe or see.

25. because maybe i forgot how to.

26. world mental health day—because, maybe, i
    just needed a day to remind myself that
    everything will be okay.. or a day, to remind
    me of the state of my mental health.

ten: what is love?

generally i assume i write odes
about certain something's
or a certain someone—later
i realize i never did, or i
realize my memory is shit.
i realize i might have lost my chance.
i wonder where they've all went.
i wonder if i'll remember them;
their name, their face, their scent.
if not, will they find a way
back to the places we fell
in love, with one another,
will they wait for me to
come around again. // ;

.do they long for me
      this much?

eleven: lullaby

how brave of you to let me in.
again. how many times have
you been broken.. again?
how patient of you to love again.
  to let love win, again.
however, i can't promise
i won't let you down.
    again.

  however,
  i promise
    i'll try.
again.

twelve: pride

here's to the honey in you
to the bittersweet in me;
i've shed this blood
so romantically—so viciously quiet.
here's to a moment of silence

i've poured and poured my soul; again
here's to epiphanies.

there was never a we.
there was you all
and there was me—in this war
likely to succeed,
unlike me to surrender.
trying, n dying to breathe poetry
to rise in the light of day
to subconsciously exist cautiously.
ascending towards freedom
praying for a breather

breathes deeply

do you see my pain?
do i seem like prey?
empathy,   be the reason
you're still standing.

we are not the same—i've lived
more lives than you.

i have less pride than you.

i'm extraterrestrial, i was created different.
i've been here many times before,
and i've never been defeated.

and still—
i will never
be
defeated.

thirteen: a grandma who promises.

everything is with love. everything is with light.
you will have to see it for yourself. soon you will
open your eyes as wide as they can pull, and you
will see god's hand reaching for yours. you will
see god smiling at your eminence. poke your
head toward the sky, and place your attention to
your center—then reach back; or reach within
and meditate. savor the present moment. listen
to your heart beat. take notice of the love it sings.
listen to your angel's harping and cheering for
you. observe your breath as it escapes.. slowly.
with   love and light.   with calm, with might.

and for once,
encourage everything
to fall in place

|

the way you never imagined it'd be able to.

fourteen: matrix

i have a habit of nurturing dead things,
begging for life.

shouting, "can you hear me now?"
"can you feel me now?"
desperate to find a well of holy water
and faith to help you see the light
can you see my shadow?
she's beautiful too— from a distance
most powerful when she's hidden;
i'm afraid you came far too close
see, your hands
were never supposed to meet mine, this time.
your soul was only ever supposed to stop by,
and check on me for no longer than a moment.
we said our final goodbyes,
at least a couple of life times ago
i remember this energy clearly.

why won't you go away for good?

how don't you know
we're no good for each other?
with your sun in pisces and my scorpio moon
we will only keep drowning one another.

is it me who keeps calling?
or is it me who keeps answering your cry?

i'm ashamed i couldn't bring myself to say no.
i couldn't bare to see you look so lonely
knowing how well we fit together.
i'm afraid i brought you back into this world;

this matrix, this pattern.

do you still like to run away from everything
you're too familiar with?
are you still convinced
you aren't finished learning me yet?
as if there are different dimensions.
this love, is one too many dimensions for me
sometimes i feel too alive..
so alive i can't breathe or sleep at night.

fifteen: patience

amidst the fire, rise a flame
luminous and effervescent.
i stare with admiration
and wonder. and wander.
i want to be this way.
mystical and magic.
i want to prey on you.

|

look away for a second;
feel my prayer surround you.
fill your spirit with trust.
i am here to help.
you will see me
go the distance
to love.
to dance.
to smile.

|

show me how to pray.

|

all that is yours,
will, all ways, be present.
no pursuit required.
only consistency.

|

but when?
i want love now.

|

when you're ready, and able, to trust
some one else's intentions—for you.

sixteen: transition

lately, i've been having
to remind people about me.
about the way i move
and about my clairvoyance.
i've had to remind myself—that
sometimes we need time apart
from the people we love most.
especially, if we feel we need space, inside.
sometimes i have to tell myself
it's okay to start over
and to get up
and to leave.
and to move   on.
and to move forward.
to promise myself not to give up
when things feel too hard to bare;
like gloomy weather and rejection.
like mother earth cleansing herself
and being misunderstood,

like we don't break her heart everyday. like
funerals on sunday morning instead of church.
like god forbid,
god forgot to save us too—
like the sadness the devil
never warned you about.
like, when did this get here?
this empty feeling? this depression?

lately, i feel like i've been surrounded by people
i have to pretend to be
something i'm not, around.
to pretend i'm happy to be around.
to people who suppress my feelings.
people i have to explain myself to.
"i'm not like you; see i'm depressed.
i can't fake turn up
when there's a hell inside my head.
i can't act like everything is okay,
even if i understand why it can't be.

i can't always accept
the things i don't see.

like, why is all the pressure on me?"
all i wanted was to fulfill a purpose.
had no clue i'd be this tested.
have no clue if i ever pass.
can hardly say i mind failing.

lately, i've been too exhausted
to blend in.

tired of putting up a fight
with my intuition.
tired of apologizing
for the need of space
during transition.

lately, i'm just okay
with being alone.

seventeen: all is well

yesterday i was referred to as a "black woman."
wasn't asked my name,
wasn't said directly to me—
but, was directed at me with alarm.
eyes, never taking a moment to drift.
in that moment, i wondered what all
it would take to become invisible.
to walk away as if it had never happened.
to leave trauma on the table
for the busboy to get rid of.
my shadow has become frightening.

yesterday i was referred to as a "black woman."
in the kind of way you refer
to your homes mouse problem.
in the kind of way that implies displeasure.
but this time   i   stared back.
i looked a man so deeply in the eyes
he couldn't help but fend off.
couldn't pray hard enough
to become invisible.

although i wish him well,
(her well, them well)
i can't help but hope
he carry that karma home with him.

eighteen: shame

what have we done to the world?
and what have we become,
or what have we
forgotten
about ourselves?
haven't we any thanks
for the resources
we have access to
for remedy?
have we lost touch
with what our soul needs?
is our spirit void of course?
as if the sun doesn't rise each mourning
to remind us of all that we've got?
you see this sky
wasn't made to be ignored.
she been courteous enough
to let us stay for so long.
too long without a thanks
or a bit of gratitude.
she could have decided not to,

many moons ago.

everyday she is made of our reflection,
both our two toned personalities.

are we too intimidated to heal?

have we become too comfortable
dancing with the devil,
because her promises sound exceptional?
are we conflicted?
have you ever wondered
why there's so much hate in our heart
and discomfort in our ego?
haven't you wondered why
we react with fear?
with panic?
with judgment?
with pride.
why we react

always
without accountability.

nineteen: absolutely

1. there was you and her,
and there was i—
laying alone in my uncertainty and despair.
i felt really ugly inside; but still i waited
and still i stayed.
and still i wonder
do you notice the little things?
how much longer til' you're home?
you know you're always welcomed here.
i miss you;
how much do you miss me
when you're gone?

if ever—you truly are gone.

\

will you stop taking the sun and stars with you?
when you're gone, i can't feel the warmth here.

\ \

i lay,   wondering does she feel it too?
the poison?   the pain?
the emptiness?   the rage?

\ \ \

are we fools for loving you the way we do?
for never letting go? for holding you near
on one another's   off day?

is there something i am missing?
like her pretty?   or her brains?
or her wholeness?   or her sane?
am i missing   god's   blessing?
or   are you   no good   for me?

i'm a destruction to myself.

–

2. there was her and i,
and there was you—
playing a loser's game.
with your finest cigar
and your little bit of change.
your smile far too convincing.
i was foolish to think you cared
with your grime, and your deceit,
and your constant struggle;
to be or not to be.

\

don't be foolish.
come back to me.

\\

you're foolish to believe
she cares for you.

-

3. there was you and i,
and there was her—playing
a lover's game. relaxing
in ecstasy. using
your change
your heart
your being
 at her convenience.

disregarding your efforts;
bruising your confidence.
i'm still unsure why
you   hurt   for her.

there was something
you were missing

there was something
she never gave

there is something
you'll never secure

her sincerity.
her absolute.
her trust.

    -

4. i'm here still //
    whenever you miss home.

twenty: black affinity

why   do you   bring me
so much pain? how—can
you bring   me   so much pain?
have you gathered this waste
alongside the road? where is the
soul i met?   where is your heart?
is it there?   is it near?   is it   possible
i've chased it away? is it possible
for us   to go back   to the same?
or the way   i recognize   us most.

when you loved me most.
when you meant what you said
and your promises meant the most to me.

—without the blues
there would be no jazz. and
tonight i feel a groove comin'.

i want the light dimmed
and the moon bright.
i want whatever high seas
god suggested she had brewing.
i want the mood birthed
from sex and sass.
i want whatever feels
significantly intimate.

i want love.

i wanna sing about an
unordinary love.
i wanna dance 'til sunup.

ain't that what we here for?
ain't that what we need?
a little love to set us free?
a desire for an unusual kind of freedom?
a black marriage for us all to believe in?

what will it take for us to believe
in one another? you in me, me in you.

twenty one: careful

teach me what it means
to be   "careful."
teach me what it means
to be   "in love."
i want to learn how to be
the least amount of careful
in the most amount of love.

teach me how to be patient.
teach me how to manifest an idea.

i want to learn how to be patient
manifesting   the idea   of you.

tell me how   you   celebrate me.

tell me how you   thought me
        into existence.

tell me how you brought me
        to life.

twenty two: last night

Last night i forgave you
in my dreams.

You seemed a bit lonely you,
seemed a bit confused.
seems like you been waiting
to let me in
on something?

i've been wondering
who you've been
these days. how you
holding up? are you still
trying to find a way to
appreciate the moment,
better?you still apologizing
for not knowing any
better? for not knowing
how to stay put? you
still distracted by the
same things?

you still hurting
from the same things?

If there's one thing i know,
you haven't been the same
since you lost your control
over me,
since you lost my love.

They say being away from home
too long can make you a bit crazy.
can make you forget who you are.
can make you wanna start from scratch.

We took a quicker ride
than you thought
it would be. but—you
fooled me into believing
it didn't mean the same to you.
made me a bit crazy.
made me, forget who i was.
made me.. start from scratch.

Don't, mean to open pandora's box,
but.. since this is a dream, and all,

Did it all mean anything to you?
was the ride okay? not too
bumpy? not too safe?
did you feel it right away?
did you fall right away
    like i did?

Sometimes i have these dreams
where you're doing okay, but
mostly i notice you're misplaced,
still. always in places you were
    never supposed to find.
like my heart, like, my mind.
like, remember that time
you seen me outside the club,
holding another woman's hand.
after i, left the man before.
all in love with the night and
the sins that came after.

i wouldn't dare relive
   the sins
that came after.
yet, somehow,
 i still lose myself
in finding my way
to   relive   you.

Since when do you go here?
won't you look away
so   i don't have to?

My eyes all locked in with yours.
my mouth all..   nervous.
my mouth all.. fuck you.

You   all—in love with
the ways my hips move.
you all, aye.. i miss you.
   i laugh. "yeah aight."

but,   maybe
i missed you too.

who you were
when i first met you.
who i wish you stayed.
wish your face
never came up in my dream.
wish i never thought of you.
wish i could make it make sense.
help me   make sense   of this?

help me forget.
  help me forget.
help me..
    forget.

Last night i forgave you.
  you seemed a bit lonely.

twenty three: my grandma forgot to say

nobody tells you how to survive
as a black woman.
so, let me learn you a lesson
\ you are a threat
on every point of the map. \
you are love in its purest form.
all unapologetic, all unconditional.
always too compassionate.
\ sometimes, too forgiving. \
but never, too afraid
to show up.

black women,
you are everything
they believed you wouldn't be.
\ you are gorgeous,
even through the suffering. \
you needn't forget why.
you hold the world together.
thank you for your mercy.
\ you are the strongest form of human. \

twenty four: skin

i heard trayvon died
from a skin disease.

heard his mama forgot
to tell him it was deadly,
heard he knew so anyway though
heard he birthed a nation
heard he turned niggas woke
heard his species was endangered
heard it's better to live a good life
than a full one. they made us believe
any life is better than the black one.
the brown one.   the tan one.
poor young man   was too dark
for his own good. heard
he was shot in the heart by
a lighter man—whose skin
got melanin too. shit, i heard
he got away with it. heard
he sold the gun for over
a couple hunna thousand,

heard the law turnt a blind eye.
he seem to be
gettin' away with it.

heard he got ptsd.
heard he livin' protected.
heard he go to bed
scared for his life.
heard he got no guilt.
heard he don't really need
none, though. most of them
lighter men get away with things.

killing black men
    ain't pose to be one of them.

killing black kids
    ain't pose to be one of them.

killing black people
    ain't supposed to be okay.

twenty five: are we lost?

how do we justify our faith
when we feel betrayed by god?
how do we question our god
with sincerity? are we wrong
for having curiosity? are we
no good because—we are lost?

will god help us
    find our way back?

i want to know how to fall
out of love with a person who
was taken from me. i want
the chance to say i'm proud of you
for all your grit and all your
 heart, even after it was all stolen
from you. i wish you wasn't
   stolen from me.
i want to give credit to fate for
all the shit that'll never make sense
to me. but this trauma that was

passed down to me will never
go away at the rate i've been
  thinking about suicide.
i be wanting to ask my demons
every question about how
beautiful my suicide would be.
paint the picture please.
i be wanting to forget all the
misery i've been accompanied
by. i be wondering where i go
sometimes, i mean, i never
thought about who i was til
i had my body stolen from me.
had my body chewed up
and
spit out.
had my body misused
by a devil it wasn't
intended for.

a soul food of demons.
 a lesson i wasn't prepared for.
  or hoping, or asking for.

wasn't craving. the questions
came soon after. i wish
i knew where i came from.
 i wish i had a place to make
it back home to. earlier i
thought about the boat that
sailed over. i wonder which
ocean was sorrowful enough
to feel the need to swallow it.
she forgot to swallow us first.
still,   i wonder how   we made it.
and,

i
wonder why
we haven't found
our way back.

may god help
us find our way   home.

may god help us
                        stay safe / on the way.

twenty six: you   know   i do

if i told you how much i need you
i'd be the sucker in the game.
i think the meaning is beyond me.
my daddy taught me how to act.
my daddy taught me game, said
this how you—be a lady.
a lady never bugs a man.
never let's herself get played
because in this life—they gon' try
to play you. to hurt you. to
fuck you over. you can't
believe everything, you don't
know if they stand strong by
they 'word'.

if i told you, "i love you"
you might not believe it.
if i told you, "i love you"
you might think deep about it.
might think my love ain't
enough for you. might think

you've loved me harder and
you tired of using up all you got.
might be   finished trying.
i got a habit of thinking about
loving you harder. i ask how.
i say, "don't lose him."
i say, "don't fuck this up again!"
i say, "please, try harder."
i say, "say i love you."
i say, "say i love you."
i say, "say i love you!"

the words never come out.
the words you've been dying
to hear, instead i say
"i'm sorry.
you know i do.. though."

twenty seven: isis

if i was lauren
i woulda burnt the city down.
the city we were raised in,
the city we found love in
the city we   fell   for.
the city that loved you like me,
the city that robbed you from me.
the city of all illusions.
if i was lauren
i would have stayed silent.
i would've held on to
the little of our privacy left.
to the fullness of our lives.
to the seeds that were buried.
to the prayers we held together.
to the soul work we mastered.
there was so much more to master.
i know she misses
her soul mates laughter.
i would've grieved privately.
if i was lauren

i would have reminisced
on the man who loved me for me.
who married me   despite what
they had planned for us.
i would have reminisced
about the day we gave birth.
 i would have reminisced
on the man who recognized
the power in me. who chose
  to take a chance on me.
cause you know   we ain't—never
supposed   to end up   together.
niggas all   powerful   when they
together   —   they love
to keep niggas   separate.
like to keep our
   women lonely.
if i was lauren
i'd be so damn angry.
i oughtta search for the
body who stole yours.
dare anybody trying to stop me
trying to test my patience.

ain't no   chill   in me.
i could give a fuck about leisure
if i was lauren
i'd start a war.
i'd start a riot if it meant
niggas might   wake up.
  might   start   to
open
their
eyes
on the niggas
god is sending
down to 'em.
on the niggas
meant to save us.

if i was lauren
i would've stood
at the podium
searching for god.
speaking at god in question.
speaking at god with passion.
speaking at god in panic.

speaking foreign to him,
or her, in my native tongue .
: god,   what the fuck is this?
: god,   why   me?

if i was lauren
i might have to ask,
"how you hate
on tha nigga
who love him
some you?"

"how you feel
knowing you
assassinated
an angel?"
"   do you
feel complete?"

i'm thankful

lauren got this.

im thankful
lauren prays.
i'm thankful
lauren knew
ermias' role
in this world.
i'm thankful
lauren loved
him into his
 godliness.
i'm thankful
lauren stood
on ten toes
to remind us
who we she fell
in love with.
i'm thankful
lauren shared
him with us.

i'm thankful
for lauren's
 strength.

twenty eight: my new therapist is latinx

i finally gave in and decided to get a therapist.
thought it'd make sense to release some shit. shit
i been holding on to for a minute now. shit i cant
forget. but for a minute we been playing tag on
the phone—so i'm wondering if it's some sort
of sign. what sign, i don't know, but part of me
—doesn't want to go anyway. something i've
been afraid of since forever. since everybody acts
well, i guess i should too.   i try to fit the
perfect mold. i been wanting life to make sense.

was i loved or   was i not.
was it love,   or was it not?
i can't make it out.

i've been too afraid to question the truth.
i've been too dependent on the idea of life
being too good to me. i like to think about
the good times more than ever lately. i go
back like fifteen years. i go, fifteen years ago
i was ten.   fuck,   what was i doing when

i was ten? what was i thinking back
then? did i have the slightest clue?
did i think life could get any better?

i used to walk home from school every
day. i would stop by the liquor store
on my way there. i'd wave at the clerk
who felt like family because he never
stopped being shocked about how
much i'd grown since   last week. he
told me to enjoy being young. you
can make all the excuses in the world
on why you haven't done the work,
when you're young. you can get away.
please enjoy your life. and shit,   i tried to.
i really did, my environment just
didn't really allow me too. always had
to think about everybody but my
damn self. had to shelf my feelings
away. had to worry. i worried about my
future often.   where i'd go. who
i'd meet. wondered if i'd find a
partner, a bit more healthy. a bit

more in love with me. wonder why it
took me twenty plus years to realize, my
daddy was never really that "in love"
with my mother. never put her first
even when she was his first real love.
the first woman to love him like
he was one of her own. looked at
him beyond skin. looked at him
with hope. hope he'd turn out to
be something different than what
she was used to. she was used to the
kind of dudes who would fall in love
but still leave—then couldn't help
but come find her because of her
impression on things. she was used
to the kind of guys who were easily
influenced or afraid. she knew
she couldn't be with a man who
was too afraid to be challenged.
she was sixteen when she gave her
life for him. she let him be that one.
he never put her first. he never
made her his one and only. just kept

her at bay.　just in case.　　bae, just
in case— be patient with me,　　he'd say.
imma figure it out. so i figure
he never did. and i figure i still
can't wrap my head around it.
still stuck on stupid. still stuck on it.
i had a nightmare the other night
where i couldn't get my son to say
he loved me back. i think maybe cause
it's been a year and i still ain't said it yet.
still tryna learn how to. still wonder
if i start now, will he say it back?
will he understand me? i think about
my fears and for me it's not failure.
it's never being known for the truth
and never fully showing my loved ones
the best parts of me. the parts where
i can love harder than nobody they've
ever known. the part of life i understand
the most is—we may never meet again.
this may be something temporary. so
why not leave, the best of impressions.
why not love on one another. i think

maybe i, learned that from my mother.
maybe i, watched.. then learned how to
give people reassurance—everything
will always fall in it's place. that's what
she used to say til—everything fell apart.
ain't heard no talk about later or god
no more. ain't heard her talk
much about anything really.
sometimes i say, i seen my daddy
the other day and she say, "oh yeah?"
i say, yeah.. he doing a little better.
but she never really respond to it. so
i said.. maybe it's time to see someone.
someone who might could help me.
somebody colored, so they can be
a little fucked up too. said.. nah
it's definitely time to seek help.
can't go a day without talking
about the difference. between us
and them. between now and then.
now would probably be the best
time to seek reformation. now
that   i notice   the difference.

twenty nine: grandma knows

when the hurt is over,
i say, thank god. i say
today i'm going to find
my way to abuela's
house. i always assume
she'll make it til morning.
when the mourning is
over due—i say, i'm sorry.
i give myself a pass for
being unable to feel things
in the exact moment they
come along. when the
tears make their way, i let
them come. i let them
find their way out. i
hold the door open.
when the questions begin,
i always start with a why?
then a how, then a where.
i wonder where i fit the
best. i say, but where

exactly do i belong?
i say, where exactly
do they   want us?
i say, and wasn't this
our   home first?
first homes are never
the best of choices.
i say, i've got no home
to be. i say, let me go
check on   abuela.
let me make sure she
still got that faith.
 when the fear makes
its way, i say—god,
can you ride for me?
can you promise not
to switch sides on me?
can you acknowledge
that i'm near the last
level? i did the work
for you. can you help
us see it   through.
can you help us

break free. when the
people came to stay,
i wonder how they
convinced you to give
them your blessing.
and again, when they
came to raid us—to
play us out this fantasy..
to deprive us of the
american dream, where
were you to wash
them away? my
abuela said, she lived
a lifetime here. a
beautiful eighty-five
years. a beautiful
nightmare. ten broken
children. one failed
marriage. a man too
high on his own
horse. disrespecting
everything they
worked on achieving

together. i ask,
when the love is
gone, is it safe to
love another. is it
okay to move on?
according to god?
since you all tight,
or whatever. she
say, i've moved on.
we all should. and
whatever may come,
will come—just be
ready. when the
anger manifests
itself, a lot of
hearts will be broken.
you have to be ready.
we were not born
to live in one place
forever. i say, that's
not the point. the
point is, we're being
misplaced again.

she say, not if
it's up to god.

god makes
no mistakes.

thirty. closing.

i began this book on
October 17, 2017.
today is July 25, 2019.
for two long years, i sat
aside and stood patient.
i housed my son for nine
long months. and as of now,
i've breastfed my son for
thirteen long months.
i haven't slept in forever.
i've been overthinking
as a hobby it seems.
i was able to start and
finish a few projects..
which is cool but i'm glad
to be done with my own.
i tried to give this one a bit
more thought.
a little less judgement
 though.
i figured i could allow
myself to feel things
and write 'em down.
i figure, whatever come

to the surface should
be deemed worthy..
even if it all sounds
or seems the same.
sometimes, that's how
this healing shit goes..
right? you feel the same
things twice or more.

your investment
means the world to me.
your return will be
intentional and
rewarding.

do   something.
be   something.
        mean   something.

question everything
  you think you know.
unlearn your lessons,
  meet your wounds again.
make sure you're healed,   forreal.

  lastly,   have empathy   with yourself.

Made in the USA
Monee, IL
31 October 2019